About the Series

It might almost be said that the most enchanting part of baseball lies not in watching it, but in remembering it. No sport lends itself so effortlessly to memory, to conversation; no sport has so graphic an afterlife in its statistics; nor has any been photographed so thoroughly and excitingly.

Beginning with 1901, the year most historians identify as the dawn of baseball's "modern era," there have been nearly 90 seasons, with no two even remotely alike. The mention of a certain year can evoke the memory of a team, the image of a man, or the drama of a moment. For many fans, it is all so vivid that baseball has become for them a long calendar of historical events.

Every season begins the same, with everyone equal on Opening Day, stirring with optimism and anticipation. And every season ends the same way, with surprises and disappointments, among teams and individuals both. No baseball summer has even been, or can be, dull. No baseball summer has ever been forgotten, for every one has been a source of stories and numbers, many of which have become part of our national folklore.

It is the purpose of this series of books to make it all happen one more time.

The Bantam Baseball Collection

#2

American League

Most Valuable Players

Written by
Donald Honig

Packaged by Angel Entertainment, Inc.
and M.I.B. Baseball Enterprises, Inc.

BANTAM BOOKS
TORONTO • NEW YORK • LONDON • SYDNEY • AUCKLAND

Acknowledgment

Much of the material in this book was collected with the help of AWARD VOTING by Bill Deane, published by the Society For American Baseball Research. Mr. Deane is senior research associate at the National Baseball Hall of Fame and Museum in Cooperstown, New York.

American League Most Valuable Players

A Bantam Book / April 1989

Book design / production by Karen J. Stelzl

ISBN 0-553-27980-7

PRINTED IN THE UNITED STATES OF AMERICA

0 9 8 7 6 5 4 3 2 1

Contents

1959:	Nelson Fox	60
1960:	Roger Maris	62
1961:	Roger Maris	64
1962:	Mickey Mantle	68
1963:	Elston Howard	70
1964:	Brooks Robinson	72
1965:	Zoilo Versalles	74
1966:	Frank Robinson	76
1967:	Carl Yastrzemski	78
1968:	Denny McLain	80
1969:	Harmon Killebrew	82
1970:	Boog Powell	84
1971:	Vida Blue	86
1972:	Dick Allen	88
1973:	Reggie Jackson	90
1974:	Jeff Burroughs	92
1975:	Fred Lynn	94
1976:	Thurman Munson	96
1977:	Rod Carew	98
1978:	Jim Rice	100
1979:	Don Baylor	102
1980:	George Brett	104
1981:	Rollie Fingers	106
1982:	Robin Yount	108
1983:	Cal Ripkin	110
1984:	Willie Hernandez	112
1985:	Don Mattingly	114
1986:	Roger Clemens	116
1987:	George Bell	118
1988:	Jose Canseco	120

Introduction

The designation speaks for itself: Most Valuable Player. It has become baseball's most distinguished and prestigious award, and every November, fans avidly await the selections in each league.

There were several false starts in the creation of an MVP Award before the honor as we know it today was formulated on December 11, 1930, at the winter meetings of the Baseball Writers Association of America (BBWAA). The first attempt at an official award was put forward by the Chalmers Motor Company in 1910. As a promotional gimmick, the company announced that it would give one of its cars to the major league player with the highest batting average. A year later, the company changed the award by offering a car to the player in each league who proved himself to be "the most important and useful player to his club and to the league at large in point of deportment and value of services rendered." The decision was to be made by a vote of one baseball writer from each city in each league.

The Chalmers award remained in existence for four years, fading out in 1914. The National League winners were: Frank Schulte of the Cubs, Larry Doyle of the Giants, Jake Daubert of the Dodgers, and Johnny Evers of the Braves. The American League winners were: Ty Cobb of the Tigers, Tris Speaker of the Red Sox, Walter Johnson of the Senators and Eddie Collins of the Athletics.

In 1922, the American League formed a Trophy Committee to select annually a player "who is of greatest all-around service to his club and credit to the sport during each season." There were some absurdities in the voting

1

process that doomed this award from the beginning: the writers had to select one player from each team, player-managers (a fairly common breed then) were ineligible for consideration, and no player could win the honor more than once. The votes were tabulated as follows: eight points for a first-place selection, seven for second, on down to one for eighth.

In 1924, the National League instituted its own award, with more equitable voting procedures: a writer could vote for ten players and was not limited to one player per team, player-managers were eligible, and previous winners were not ineligible.

These league awards continued through the 1928 season for the American League and 1929 for the National, when they were discontinued. One of the reasons for the end of the awards was that the winners were attempting to use them as springboards for salary increases.

The winners in the American League during these years were: George Sisler (Browns), Babe Ruth (Yankees), Walter Johnson (Senators), Roger Peckinpaugh (Senators), George Burns (Indians), Lou Gehrig (Yankees), and Mickey Cochrane (Athletics). In the National League, the winners were: Dazzy Vance (Dodgers), Rogers Hornsby (Cardinals), Bob O'Farrell (Cardinals), Paul Waner (Pirates), Jim Bottomley (Cardinals), and Rogers Hornsby (Cubs).

Beginning in 1931, the BBWAA began their selection of an MVP from each league, and it is these selections that are recognized today. From 1931 through 1937, electors were limited to one writer in each major-league city. From 1938 to 1961, this was changed to three writers in each city, and then back to two. In 1938, the value of the votes was changed to 14 points for each first-place vote a player received, nine for second, and on down to one for tenth.

Since 1931, unanimous selections have been rare. In the American League there have been six: Hank Greenberg (1935), Al Rosen (1953), Mickey Mantle (1956), Frank Robinson (1966), Denny McLain (1968), and Reggie Jackson (1973). In the National League there have been just three: Carl Hubbell (1936), Orlando Cepeda (1967), and Mike Schmidt (1980).

1931: Lefty Grove

There was never anything like him on a pitching mound–a lefthander who threw that hard. Perhaps Rube Waddell, around the turn of the century, although Connie Mack, who managed them both, wasn't so sure. But one thing was for certain–there was never a more cantankerous character on the pitching mound than Robert Moses (Lefty) Grove. He is a man whose will to win has been described as "terrifying." His spitfire left arm could pump blinding fast balls for nine innings without letup. Nor is this merely a convenient figure of speech, for in 1931 he started 30 games for the pennant-winning Philadelphia Athletics and completed 27 (in his spare time he relieved 11 times).

In 1931, Grove was at his peak, with a 31-4 record and .886 winning percentage, which is about as good as a big league pitcher is going to get. (Lefty's 31 in 1931 has the same numerical symmetry to it as Roger Maris's 61 in 1961). You name it, and Lefty led in it in 1931–wins, winning percentage, earned run average (2.06), complete games, strikeouts (175), and shutouts (3).

Lefty also led the league in emotional explosions, and none was more memorable than the one that followed a 1-0 loss to the St. Louis Browns, which deprived Lefty of a new league record. With 16 consecutive wins, Grove was trying to break the American League record he co-held with Smoky Joe Wood and Walter Johnson (both set in 1912), but a misplayed fly ball in left field cost him the game.

In what evidently was a virtuoso display of post-game rage, Lefty rearranged the Athletics' clubhouse, smashing chairs, denting lockers, tearing apart uniforms. "But the next day," a teammate said, "he was all right again."

Don't be so sure: when this writer encountered the now silver-haired and allegedly mellowed Mr. Grove more than forty years later and asked about the broken 16-game streak in 1931, the old pitcher gave me a sidelong glance and said tersely, "I don't want to talk about that game."

Despite the almost untarnished brilliance of his season's work, Grove was no automatic choice as MVP, not with that Yankee bruiser Lou Gehrig slugging away in New York and Lefty's own teammate Al Simmons having the year of his life. Lou hit 46 home runs, drove in 184 runs (still the league record) and batted .341. Simmons led the league with a .390 average. But none of this prodigious hitting could eclipse the glory of a 31-4 record. Lefty won it, with Gehrig second and Simmons third.

Grove's 1931 Record

WON	LOST	PCT.	G	GS	CG	INP	HITS	BB	SO	SH	ERA
31	4	.886	41	30	27	289	249	62	175	3	2.05

Lefty Grove, Connie Mack's tempestuous non-stop winner

1932: Jimmie Foxx

"He was seventeen years old when he came into the league, and he was strong enough then. But we watched him fill out a little more each year and just keep getting stronger and stronger. It was scary, especially if you were a pitcher."

That was Chicago White Sox righthander Ted Lyons talking, and he was talking about James Emory Foxx. The youngster was born in Maryland, the same state as Babe Ruth, and the resemblance did not stop there. If anybody hit them as hard and as far as Ruth, it was Foxx, who soon became known as "the righthanded Babe Ruth," which is about as complimentary as it gets in baseball.

Jimmie's 1932 season was indeed Ruthian; in fact, the 24-year-old Philadelphia Athletics firstbaseman came near to erasing Ruth's single-season record of 60 homers by hitting 58. Connie Mack's strongboy also led with 169 runs batted in and had a .364 batting average, losing the Triple Crown only because Dale Alexander, who split his season between Boston and Detroit, edged him out with a .367 mark.

"Jimmie was a brute force at home plate," said his teammate Jimmy Dykes. "I never saw anybody crack a ball as hard, not Ruth or Gehrig or Williams. Nobody. The third baseman would all but cross himself and start praying when Jimmie stepped in there."

Lou Gehrig had another fine season in New York, with 151 RBIs and a .349 average, but finished second in the voting. Washington's Heinie Manush, who batted .342, was third.

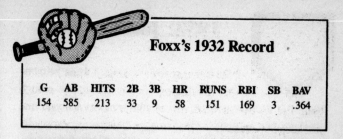

Foxx's 1932 Record

G	AB	HITS	2B	3B	HR	RUNS	RBI	SB	BAV
154	585	213	33	9	58	151	169	3	.364

Jimmie Foxx

1933: Jimmie Foxx

The country was sinking deeper into its Depression in 1933; businesses were failing and factories were closing; the unemployed, the hungry, and the homeless were everywhere.

Baseball managed to sustain itself throughout these desperate times, in some cases just barely. Among those feeling the strains of a tightening economy was Connie Mack. With diminishing attendance, Mack began selling off his higher priced stars, including Al Simmons, Mule Haas, and Jimmy Dykes. Soon Lefty Grove, Mickey Cochrane and George Earnshaw would go, and then finally, after the 1935 season, Jimmie Foxx.

In 1933, however, the 25-year-old Foxx was still an Athletic, and a productive one. Jimmie won his second consecutive MVP award, finishing ahead of Joe Cronin and Heinie Manush, manager-shortstop and outfielder, respectively, of the pennant-winning Washington Senators.

This year Jimmie swept the Triple Crown that had eluded him the year before, and won it emphatically. He had 48 home runs (Ruth was second with 34), 163 runs batted in (Gehrig was second with 139), and a .356 batting average (Manush was next with .336).

When Jimmie did not elevate a ball, he usually hit one-hop grounders that could tear the glove off an infielder's hand or line drives that buzzed like bumblebees. Dykes once described Jimmie's grounders as "line drives that bounce." When someone asked Herb Pennock how he pitched to Foxx, the veteran Yankee lefthander said, "I deliver the ball and then turn sideways. It presents less of a target if he happens to be hitting one my way."

Foxx's 1933 Record

G	AB	HIT	2B	3B	HR	RUNS	RBI	SB	BAV
149	573	204	37	9	48	125	163	2	.356

Lou Gehrig was not known for his quips. Nevertheless, "The Iron Man" had a succinct one for a rookie in 1938, soon after Gehrig had played in his 2,000th consecutive game. The rookie had just drawn a base on balls and trotted down to first base, where Gehrig was standing.

"Well, Lou," said the youngster, "this is my fifth consecutive game."

Gehrig looked at him with a wry smile and said, "Tired?"

Part of the Ted Williams legend is the story about the brash rookie's first spring camp with the Red Sox in 1938. When someone said to him, "Wait till you see Foxx hit." Ted supposedly replied, "Wait till Foxx sees me hit." The story went around for years, until Williams finally debunked it. "I never said it," Ted said, but then added, "but it sure does sound like me."

1934:
Mickey Cochrane

During the first three years of their stewardship of the MVP Awards, the baseball writers had voted the American League designation to a Philadelphia Athletic; in 1934 they selected a former Athletic.

In December 1933, Connie Mack sold his catcher Mickey Cochrane to the Detroit Tigers, continuing the dismantling of his 1929-31 pennant winners. There Cochrane was immediately installed as catcher-manager. He had been considered the driving force behind those Athletics teams and what Detroit wanted as much as his playing skills was his spirited and zesty leadership. (One of Cochrane's admirers was a lead and zinc miner in northeastern Oklahoma named Mutt Mantle, who named his firstborn after him).

Taking over a powerful ball club that included Hank Greenberg, Charlie Gehringer, Goose Goslin and others, Cochrane provided "the missing ingredient," according to Greenberg.

"He couldn't stand to lose," Greenberg said. "No one likes to lose, of course, but with Mickey it was so emotional you could feel it. He took a good team and turned it into what I believe was a great one."

Cochrane could hit (his .320 lifetime average is the highest of any catcher); he was superb behind the plate; ran remarkably well for a catcher; and possessed those scorching leadership abilities. The 31-year-old Cochrane led his club to the pennant, finishing seven games ahead of the Yankees.

The 1934 vote for the American League MVP was a close one, with Cochrane edging out teammate Charlie

Gehringer by two votes. Yankee southpaw Lefty Gomez, who was 26-5, came in third.

Cochrane led the Tigers to another pennant in 1935 (plus the world championship), but thereafter his luck turned sour. He suffered a mental breakdown in 1936 and missed much of the season. Then in May 1937, he was beaned so severely by New York's Bump Hadley that he never played again.

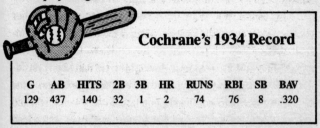

Cochrane's 1934 Record

G	AB	HITS	2B	3B	HR	RUNS	RBI	SB	BAV
129	437	140	32	1	2	74	76	8	.320

Mickey Cochrane

1935:
Hank Greenberg

No great slugger ever stood at home plate more commandingly than Hank Greenberg. At nearly 6'4" and over 200 pounds, the Detroit powerhouse stood erect in the batter's box, bat cocked menacingly and confidently.

"All great hitters are confident at the plate and they show it," said Paul Richards, one-time teammate of Greenberg's. "Greenberg was, I think, an extreme case of it. Not only did he know he could hit, but I think he enjoyed it more than most. There was always a little bit of the sandlot youngster in him, dying to put the slug on one."

In 1935, in helping to pound the Tigers to a second consecutive pennant, Big Henry put the slug on all season long, leading the league with 36 home runs and a mammoth 170 runs batted in, while batting .328. Greenberg's RBI total suggests a particularly hard-hitting season in the American League, but this was not the case; nearest to the 24-year-old Tiger star in this category was Lou Gehrig's 119, a whopping differential of 51.

"Hank loved driving in runs," teammate Charlie Gehringer said. "He got a bigger kick out of driving in runs than he did hitting homers. He once told me he wished there was a breakfast cereal called 'RBIs.' If there was, he said he'd eat them every morning."

Greenberg was the league's MVP by a comfortable margin. Runner-up was Red Sox righthander Wes Ferrell, a 25-game winner. Cleveland outfielder Joe Vosmik, who batted .348, was a distant third.

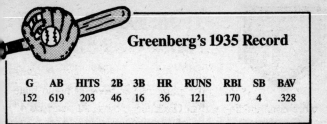

Greenberg's 1935 Record

G	AB	HITS	2B	3B	HR	RUNS	RBI	SB	BAV
152	619	203	46	16	36	121	170	4	.328

Hank Greenberg

1936: Lou Gehrig

How fierce was the competition for the Most Valuable Player trophy in the American League in the hard-hitting, star-studded 1930s? Well, despite one superb season after another, Lou Gehrig won it only once. In 1934, when he won the Triple Crown with 49 home runs, 165 runs batted in, and .363 batting average, he finished fifth in the voting. But finally, in 1936, the New York Yankees' "Iron Man" took his only MVP award, finishing eight votes ahead of Chicago's Luke Appling, who batted a lofty .388. Well behind in third place was Cleveland's Earl Averill, who batted .378 and had 232 hits.

Gehrig, in his twelfth full year as Yankee firstbaseman, blasted 49 home runs (the league's best), drove in 152 runs, and batted .354, all the while adding to his remarkable consecutive game hitting streak. Lou's thunderous hitting helped the Yankees to what was the first of four straight pennants and world championships. With six regulars batting .300, the Yankees rolled to an easy pennant, finishing 19 1/2 games in front of the Tigers. Joining the New Yorkers this year was rookie center fielder Joe DiMaggio.

Gehrig was one of the most prolific RBI men in baseball history, averaging nearly one per game throughout his career–1,990 for 2,164 games. He shares with Jimmie Foxx the major league record for most consecutive years of 100 or more RBIs–13, and in seven of those years he drove in over 150.

Gehrig's consecutive game streak ended at 2,130 on May 2, 1939 when he was forced from the lineup for the first time since June 1, 1925, by the onset of a rare disease, amyotrophic lateral sclerosis, a killer that gradually strangles the muscles. He died on June 2, 1941, a few weeks before his thirty-eighth birthday.

Yankee manager Joe McCarthy, who in his many years in the game, managed at one time or another, Roger Hornsby, Babe Ruth, Joe DiMaggio and Ted Williams, and who was not prone to playing favorites, once confided to a writer that Gehrig had been his favorite.

"Why not?" McCarthy said. "He showed up every day, he hit the ball, he never made any trouble, he never complained. A nice boy."

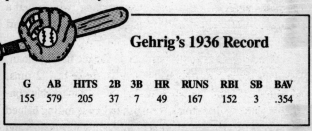

Gehrig's 1936 Record

G	AB	HITS	2B	3B	HR	RUNS	RBI	SB	BAV
155	579	205	37	7	49	167	152	3	.354

Lou Gehrig, "The Iron Man"

1937:
Charlie Gehringer

They called him "The Mechanical Man" because he did it all on a ball field and did it with seeming effortlessness; and they called him "The Quiet Man" because while he was doing it, he seldom uttered a word. Reticent, efficient, almost flawless—that was Detroit's second baseman Charlie Gehringer, the American League's MVP in 1937.

Some people felt New York's Joe DiMaggio might have won it in 1937, with his .345 batting average, 167 RBIs, and league-leading 46 home runs. Others felt that Gehringer's teammate Hank Greenberg, with 183 RBIs, should have won it. In fact, DiMaggio was a close second in the voting to Charlie, while Greenberg was a distant third.

Boosting Charlie to the prestigious award was his league-high .371 batting average and his 209 hits. He was one of four Tigers to collect 200 or more hits this year, the others being Greenberg, and outfielders Pete Fox and Gerald Walker. There was, however, another dimension to Charlie's award.

"He was, year after year," Jimmy Dykes said, "one of the most consistently excellent players I ever saw. Not only did he get the big hit in the late innings, but when you looked back at how the rallies were made, you always saw that he had a key hit right in the middle. And in the field he did it all and he never looked like he broke a sweat doing it either."

Charlie had a habit at home plate that exasperated pitchers: very often he would not swing until he had two strikes.

"He'd spot you two strikes," fastballer Wes Ferrell said, "and you always thought you had him. But he'd end up lining a hit off of you. He was as tough to fan as any man in the league."

Why did Charlie take those strikes?

"It seemed to make me concentrate more," the Quiet Man said. "With two strikes you don't go after a bad ball, you don't overswing. You're just a better hitter."

Gehringer's 1937 Record

G	AB	HITS	2B	3B	HR	RUNS	RBI	SB	BAV
144	564	209	40	1	14	133	96	11	.371

Charlie Gehringer

1938: Jimmie Foxx

It was another banner year for overachievers in the American League: Joe DiMaggio drove in 140 runs and batted .324; Hank Greenberg hit a monumental 58 home runs; 19-year-old Bob Feller had 240 strikeouts (most in the league since 1913); and Bobo Newsom was a 20-game winner for the seventh-place St. Louis Browns. But the MVP designee, and by a large margin, was Boston's Jimmie Foxx.

In winning the distinction for the third time, the slugger with the iron-plated body hit 50 home runs, drove in 175 runs (fourth highest total in major league history), and won the batting crown with a .349 average.

Greenberg's 58 home runs did not even earn him second place in the voting, which went to Bill Dickey, the great catcher of the pennant-winning Yankees.

Even though 35 of Foxx's 50 home runs were hit at Fenway Park, where the left-field wall was near and neighborly, everyone agreed Jimmie did not need the wall to enhance his home run total.

"When Jimmie kissed it," Wes Ferrell said, "it was goodbye, whether you were playing in Fenway Park or Yellowstone Park."

Those were the stories they told about Foxx's strength and his power. Now they were starting to add another: Jimmie's love of the night life, his consumption of whiskey, his free-spending. In a few years, this lifestyle began to show even on Jimmie's robust constitution. By the time he was 34, his career was for all intents and purposes over. It's a sad story, but not an unusual one for celebrities.

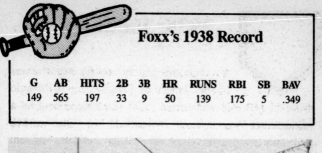

Foxx's 1938 Record

G	AB	HITS	2B	3B	HR	RUNS	RBI	SB	BAV
149	565	197	33	9	50	139	175	5	.349

Jimmie Foxx taking his rips at the Red Sox' Sarasota, Florida spring camp.

1939: Joe DiMaggio

By 1939, in just his fourth major league season, he was already a legend in the making, performing with an on-the-field splendor and exuding an off-the-field magnetism so compelling that a half century later he would still be one of the country's most admired and recognizable names.

The impeccable DiMaggio machine was never better than in 1939. Playing baseball with an all-around authority never seen before and never equaled since, he entered the month of September batting over .400. He probably would have cleared that polestar barrier, had not an eye ailment caused blurred vision and a dip in his average to a final figure of .381, his highest ever and more than enough to lead the league.

In leading the Yankees to their fourth consecutive pennant (and in October their fourth consecutive World Series victory), the 24-year-old center fielder hit 30 home runs and drove in 126 runs (in 120 games because an early-season leg injury had cost him 34 games.) He also struck out just 20 times in 462 official plate appearances, an incredible statistic for a power hitter.

With Lou Gehrig's fatal illness forcing the "Iron Man" into retirement that spring, DiMaggio became the symbol of Yankee might. The quiet young man became the team leader, an inspirational force who led by example.

"There was never a more dedicated team player than Joe," Yankee pitcher Spud Chandler said. "He was special, but he never expected special treatment. He played harder and gave more of himself than anybody else. If a guy wasn't hustling or was in some way goofing off, Joe wouldn't say anything to him, he would just stare at him, and that was enough. A frown from Joe was worth a thousand words, believe me."

In winning the first of his three MVP Awards, DiMaggio easily outdistanced Jimmie Foxx, who batted .360 and led in home runs (35), and Bob Feller, who was 24-9. Finishing fourth in the voting was a rookie, Boston's Ted Williams, who batted .327 and led the league with 145 RBIs, still the major-league record for a first-year man.

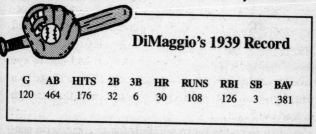

DiMaggio's 1939 Record

G	AB	HITS	2B	3B	HR	RUNS	RBI	SB	BAV
120	464	176	32	6	30	108	126	3	.381

The DiMaggio cut.

1940:
Hank Greenberg

Hank Greenberg had won the MVP Award in 1935, but then in 1937, when he drove in 183 runs, he finished only third. In 1938, when he hit 58 home runs, he again was third in the balloting. In 1940, however, he was not to be denied. Despite some high-caliber competition from Bob Feller, who was 27-11 and came within one game of pitching the Indians to the pennant, and from Joe DiMaggio, who won his second straight batting title with a .352 average, Big Henry easily outdistanced them and won his second MVP trophy.

With league-leading figures in home runs (41) and RBIs (150), plus a .340 batting average, Greenberg led the Tigers to the pennant. The big slugger added another distinction to his already glittering career when he became the first man to win an MVP Award at two different positions. Wanting to add Rudy York's home run bat to the lineup, the Tigers moved York from behind the plate, where he was a defensive liability, to first base. Before this could be done, however, the club had to persuade their star slugger to relocate in left field, which Greenberg agreed to do (but not before the Tigers had been talked into bumping up his salary by $10,000).

When it came to banging the long ball, Big Henry was a man of basics. Responding to someone who asked him to expound on the art of slugging, Greenberg said, "No one can tell you how to hit home runs. You either have the natural strength and reflexes, or you don't."

Greenberg's 1940 Record

G	AB	HITS	2B	3B	HR	RUNS	RBI	SB	BAV
148	573	195	50	8	41	129	150	6	.340

Hank Greenberg

1941: Joe DiMaggio

The 1941 American League season saw two of the most legendary talents in all of baseball history each turn in a summer of what has proven to be unsurpassed brilliance. For the electors of the Most Valuable Player, the dilemma was almost insoluble: which was the nobler achievement—Joe DiMaggio's 56-game hitting streak or Ted Williams' .406 batting average? The question has never been satisfactorily answered, although the writers gave their best opinion by selecting Joe over Ted by a vote of 291-254, 25-game winner Bob Feller was third.

The streak began on May 15 and continued for 56 games before Joe was finally lassoed in Cleveland on the night of July 17. It was a streak that both electrified and diverted the country during that tense pre-war summer. DiMaggio's hitting throughout the streak was solid and emphatic: .408 batting average, 15 home runs, 55 runs batted in. For the season as a whole, he batted .357, hit 30 home runs, and drove in a league-leading 125 runs, spearheading the Yankees to an easy pennant (they clinched on September 2, the earliest date ever). Another eye-catching DiMaggio statistic in 1941 was this: in 541 official times at bat, just 13 strikeouts.

Ballplayers are generally a tough breed to impress, but the 1941 Yankees were so dazzled by their 26-year-old center fielder that they chipped in and bought him a sterling silver humidor.

"It was our way of paying tribute to him," teammate Tommy Henrich said.

The presentation was made one night at Washington's Shoreham Hotel.

"Joe was genuinely surprised and deeply moved,' Henrich said. "He just looked around at us all like he couldn't understand why we were doing this. Finally somebody said, 'Joe, it's for showing everybody how it's supposed to be done."

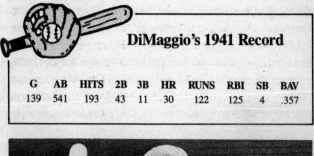

DiMaggio's 1941 Record

G	AB	HITS	2B	3B	HR	RUNS	RBI	SB	BAV
139	541	193	43	11	30	122	125	4	.357

Joe DiMaggio: nobody ever did it better, and nobody ever looked better doing it.

1942: Joe Gordon

One of the most questionable MVP selections occurred in the American League in 1942, when New York Yankee secondbaseman Joe Gordon was voted the award. It seems to have been a matter of politics.

However, there was no doubt that Gordon had turned in a superb all-around season as he helped the Yankees to the pennant: 18 home runs, 103 RBIs, .322 batting average, in addition to some acrobatic fielding that earned him the nickname "Flash." Gordon's credentials were impeccable, but the man he edged aside in the voting was a Triple Crown winner, Ted Williams, who hit 36 homers, had 137 RBIs, and a .356 batting average. (Boston's rookie shortstop Johnny Pesky was a distant third.) It was reported that some Boston writers, whom the outspoken young Williams had snapped at, got even with Ted when it came to filling out their ballots.

Gordon was a logical alternative. He had caught the eye of the writers by virtue of his strong and steady play all season. Joe looked even better because of the fall-off suffered by DiMaggio, who dropped from .357 to .305. According to one writer, Gordon led the league in "diving stops, leaping catches, and off-balance throws."

Gordon's .322 batting average was the highest of his career, and was in fact the only time he reached .300.

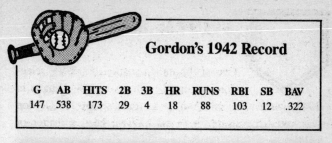

Gordon's 1942 Record

G	AB	HITS	2B	3B	HR	RUNS	RBI	SB	BAV
147	538	173	29	4	18	88	103	12	.322

Joe Gordon.

1943: Spud Chandler

Since the establishment of the MVP Awards as administered by the Baseball Writers Association in 1931, the New York Yankees have won 27 pennants (through the 1987 season), but only once has a Yankee pitcher taken the MVP designation. It wasn't Lefty Gomez or Red Ruffing, nor Vic Raschi, Eddie Lopat, or Allie Reynolds, nor the great Whitey Ford or Ron Guidry. It was Spud Chandler, in 1943, on the strength of a superb 20-4 season that included a 1.64 earned run average, at the time the lowest ever in the lively-ball era.

Chandler was a tough, gritty competitor, a man whose pre-game preparation included the stoking of his personal furies until he was ready to take the mound. That was his reputation. The Yankee righthander saw it differently.

"They said I used to sit in the clubhouse and scowl and glower," he said, "and that not until I was full of rancor was I ready to go out and pitch. Well, that just wasn't true. I was just so determined to win that it might have looked that way. But I never got what you would call mad, or disgruntled, or overbearing."

Chandler's chief competition for the MVP Award came from White Sox shortstop Luke Appling, who won the batting crown (.328) and the Tigers' Rudy York, the home run and RBI leader. Toward the end of the season, Chandler, with a 19-4 record, pitched a 14-inning 2-1 victory over the Tigers at Yankee Stadium. After the game, his catcher, Bill Dickey, said to him, "This game got you the Most Valuable Player Award. You just won it. I guarantee you that."

"Yankee pitchers," Chandler said, "had learned years

ago never to argue with anything that Bill Dickey said."

So Bill Dickey was right again, and Spud Chandler, whose .717 lifetime winning percentage is the highest in baseball history for a pitcher with 100 or more wins, became the first American League pitcher since Lefty Grove in 1931 to win the MVP Award.

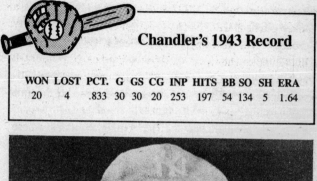

Chandler's 1943 Record

WON	LOST	PCT.	G	GS	CG	INP	HITS	BB	SO	SH	ERA
20	4	.833	30	30	20	253	197	54	134	5	1.64

Spud Chandler

1944: Hal Newhouser

With World War II having depleted the big league rosters, 1944 became the season of unrecognizable names, the lame and the halt, the green and the overcooked. The St. Louis Browns won the pennant (the only one they ever took) and a pre-war mediocrity, which had been 8-17 the year before, suddenly became a lion with a carcass. Detroit's 23-year-old lefthander, Hal Newhouser, feasted on the ghosts and the pretenders and rang up a handsome 29-9 record. It earned the southpaw the Most Valuable Player Award, as he and teammate Dizzy Trout (27-14) came within a game of pitching the Tigers to the pennant.

Newhouser barely edged out Trout for the MVP title, 236 votes to 232 (Browns shortstop Vern Stephens came in third). Despite Newhouser's higher winning percentage, a lot of people felt Trout should have been MVP. The righthander had pitched more innings, had more complete games, more shutouts, and a lower earned run average. The glamor of Newhouser having won nearly 30 games, however, finally dazzled enough writers to assure him the trophy.

Newhouser's 1944 Record

WON	LOST	PCT.	G	GS	CG	INP	HITS	BB	SO	SH	ERA
29	9	.763	47	34	25	312	264	102	187	6	2.22

1945: Hal Newhouser

The talent was still pretty thin in 1945, and taking full advantage of it, Detroit's Hal Newhouser helped himself to another season of lusty pitching and won his second straight Most Valuable Player Award. More important, he pitched his team to the pennant.

The slim lefthander, known as much for his irascible temperament on the mound (he glared and scowled at teammates who dared bobble a ball while he was pitching) as for his fastball, posted a 25-9 record and scintillating 1.81 earned run average. But again, he was a flashlight in a roomful of glittering candles. Newhouser's teammate, secondbaseman Eddie Mayo, was runner-up in the balloting, and Yankee secondbaseman George Stirnweiss was third, despite leading the league in runs, hits, triples, stolen bases, batting (.309), and slugging.

"He wasn't a bad pitcher," one teammate said of Newhouser, "but he could just as easily have won two awards that year—Most Valuable and Least Popular. He was as irritating a player as I have ever known. If an error was made behind him you could see the smoke coming out of his ears, and if you didn't get him enough runs he'd sit in the dugout and sulk."

Despite the fact that Newhouser won 26 games in 1946, when all the stars had returned, his reputation today is pretty much that of a wartime player. With his prickly personality, one might say he was a cactus among the cornstalks.

33

Newhouser's 1945 Record

WON	LOST	PCT.	G	GS	CG	INP	HITS	BB	SO	SH	ERA
25	9	.735	40	36	29	313	239	110	212	8	1.81

Hal Newhouser

1946: Ted Williams

The greatest hitter in baseball history was in his fifth season before he finally won his first MVP Award. After having been "politicked" out of the honor in 1942, Ted Williams went into military service for three years, returned in 1946 and came out swinging. The 27-year-old Red Sox slugger ripped into American League pitching with a .342 batting average, 38 home runs, and 123 runs batted in. His RBI total was curtailed by 156 bases on balls, second at the time to Babe Ruth's 170 in 1923. (Ted's on-base percentage in 1946 was .496).

"Why pitch to him?" Washington manager Ossie Bluege said. "He was only going to beat your brains out. It got to the point where sometimes I'd hope the guy in front of him would hit a double so I would have the excuse to put Ted on first."

Williams' hitting was so ferocious that in June, after he had cracked three home runs in the first game of a doubleheader against Cleveland, the Indians manager Lou Boudreau, in desperation, devised "the Williams shift." This tactic positioned everyone but the left fielder and third baseman on the right side of the diamond. The stubborn Williams refused to hit to left field (as Boudreau suspected he would) and kept swinging away into the teeth of the shift. It cost him many base hits and in later years he regretted his stubbornness.

Placing second on the voting that year was two-time winner Hal Newhouser, while Ted's teammate, secondbaseman Bobby Doerr was third. With the Red Sox winning the pennant in 1946, their shortstop Johnny Pesky was fourth,

Washington's batting champion Mickey Vernon (.353) was fifth, and finishing a puzzling sixth in the voting was Cleveland's Bob Feller. Feller, the greatest pitcher of his era, who was never to win an MVP Award, was 26-15, hurled ten shutouts, and fanned a record 348 batters.

"I would liked to have won it at least once," Feller said, then added philosophically, "but that's what happens when you're playing at the same time as Williams and DiMaggio."

Williams' 1946 Record

G	AB	HITS	2B	3B	HR	RUNS	RBI	SB	BAV
150	514	176	37	8	38	142	123	0	.342

1947: Joe DiMaggio

Joe DiMaggio won his third MVP prize in 1947. But even Joe must have been embarrassed when the results were announced. Certainly, the Yankee center fielder had produced a fine year—20 home runs, 97 RBIs, .315 batting average as he led his team to the pennant. However, the class of the league that year was clearly Boston's Triple Crown winning Ted Williams (32 homers, 114 RBIs, .343 batting average).

When all the votes had been tabulated, it was DiMaggio 202, Williams 201. Compounding this crime against good judgment was the fact that one Boston writer, nursing a grudge against Williams, omitted the name of the Triple Crown winner from his ballot entirely. Williams described the offending writer, Mel Webb as "a grouchy old guy, a real grump, and we didn't get along." When the voting was announced, Ted acknowledged his great rival in New York by saying, "There's no disgrace in losing to Joe DiMaggio."

For DiMaggio, now 32 years old, it was two post-war seasons in a row that had not measured up to his pre-war achievements. Joe would recoup in 1948 and 1949 with some outstanding slugging; but it was apparent now that the Joe DiMaggio of legend was the one who had played from 1936-1942.

Third in the voting was Cleveland's manager—shortstop Lou Boudreau, who a year later would do it all.

Ted Williams, Opposite

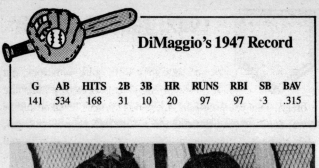

DiMaggio's 1947 Record

G	AB	HITS	2B	3B	HR	RUNS	RBI	SB	BAV
141	534	168	31	10	20	97	97	3	.315

Ted Williams (left) and Joe DiMaggio in 1941. Ted has just belted the ninth-inning home run that won the 1941 All-Star Game for the American League.

1948: Lou Boudreau

At one time they were quite numerous, but by 1948 playing managers were a vanishing breed. This year, however, there was one in Cleveland and he was summer-long dynamo. In his seventh year as manager, shortstop Lou Boudreau was still just 30 years old as he turned in the greatest season of his big league career. Always a superb clutch performer, both in the field and at bat, Boudreau drove and led his team to a first-place tie with the Boston Red Sox, necessitating the first pennant playoff in American League history. With the skipper cracking two home runs and two singles, the Indians won the game, 8-3, and with it their first pennant since 1920.

Boudreau was the runaway choice as MVP, finishing far ahead of Joe DiMaggio (who led with 39 homers and 155 RBIs) and Ted Williams, the batting champion (.369).

Boudreau achieved career highs in batting (.355), home runs (18), and RBIs (106). He also led American League shortstops in fielding for the eighth time in nine years. Never especially fast afoot, he was uncanny when it came to playing an opposing batter, and when it came to making the big play, "he always found that extra quickness he needed," said Indians owner Bill Veeck.

"Lou was always a rah-rah type of guy,"—quoting Veeck again—"but in 1948 he was a ball of fire. I've never seen a player start the season keyed up and stay that way to the very end. It was like he was on a crusade all season long, and he led us to the world championship."

Boudreau's 1948 Record

G	AB	HITS	2B	3B	HR	RUNS	RBI	SB	BAV
152	560	199	34	8	18	116	106	3	.355

Lou Boudreau

1949: Ted Williams

Only four times in his 19-year major league career did Ted Williams play in 150 or more games in a season; 1949 was one of those seasons and it was one of his greatest. He achieved personal highs in home runs (43), runs batted in (159), hits (194), and runs scored (150). Leading the league in homers and RBIs, he missed out on a third Triple Crown, batting .3427 to George Kell's .3429. That, however, was the least of Ted's disappointments in 1949, for this was the year when the Red Sox were beaten 5-3 at Yankee Stadium on the final day of the season in a game that decided the American League pennant.

Williams was an easy winner in the MVP voting, finishing nearly 100 points ahead of Yankee shortstop Phil Rizzuto. As a matter of fact, the top seven vote-getters were members of either the Red Sox or Yankees: following Williams and Rizzuto were Yankee lefthanded reliever Joe Page, Boston pitchers Mel Parnell and Ellis Kinder, Yankee outfielder-first baseman Tommy Henrich, and Boston shortstop Vern Stephens, who tied Williams with 159 RBIs.

The Red Sox manager that year was Joe McCarthy, former long-time Yankee skipper. When asked who he thought was better, DiMaggio or Williams, Joe answered, "When I was managing the Yankees, I thought Joe was better. When I was managing the Red Sox, I thought Ted was better."

When asked if the sometimes tempermental Williams ever gave him any trouble, Joe said, "Not at all. He always obeyed orders. Of course, I only gave him one order: hit. He obeyed it just fine."

Williams' 1949 Record

G	AB	HITS	2B	3B	HR	RUNS	RBI	SB	BAV
155	566	194	39	3	43	150	159	1	.343

Ted Williams

1950: Phil Rizzuto

Beginning in 1950, the American League Most Valuable Player Award developed into an annual New York Yankee coronation, since 10 of the next 14 winners were wearers of pinstripes.

The winner in 1950 was Yankee shortstop Phil Rizzuto, who put together a pinnacle year for himself with a .324 batting average and 200 hits, as well as gluing together the Yankee infield. Standing little more than 5'6", Phil looked like the man who put the "short" into shortstop, but he played the position with marvelous agility and quickness. Few infielders ever got rid of a ball quicker. (When Yankee ace Vic Raschi was asked what his best pitch was, he replied, "The one they hit to Rizzuto.")

Following Phil in the voting was Red Sox utility man Billy Goodman. He was unable to find regular work on a team of stars, so he filled in at five different positions, got his at bats and won a batting crown (.354). Next was Yankee catcher Yogi Berra, warming up for his own assault on MVP honors.

That Rizzuto was a deserving MVP in 1950 and an exceptionally gifted player is beyond question; whether his career was of Hall of Fame quality continued to be answered in the negative for decades after his retirement, despite Phil's own electioneering and the noisy commentary of George Steinbrenner. In the wonderful world of baseball politics, it is no doubt likely that some people are opposed to Rizzuto's Hall of Fame candidacy simply because Steinbrenner is for it.

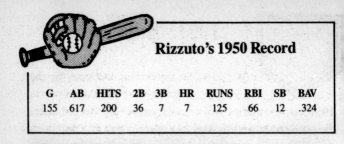

Rizzuto's 1950 Record

G	AB	HITS	2B	3B	HR	RUNS	RBI	SB	BAV
155	617	200	36	7	7	125	66	12	.324

Phil Rizzuto receiving his 1950 MVP plaque from American League president Will Harridge.

1951: Yogi Berra

According to one writer, the vote for the American League's Most Valuable Player in 1951 "proved that it was not a beauty contest." Nevertheless, the plain and homely looking Yogi Berra was a rare beauty on the ballfield. He was a shrewd handler of pitchers, a more than capable defensive catcher, a clutch-hitting slugger who whacked the ball for power and average, and a man with an uncanny batting eye (in 547 official plate appearances in 1951, he fanned just 20 times).

The future American folk hero was 26 years old when he won the first of his three MVP Awards. The first American League catcher since Cochrane in 1934 to win, Yogi batted .294, hit 27 home runs, and drove in 88 runs, while catching 141 games.

Sportswriters began creating a Yogi legend at this time, gleefully reporting his malapropisms and on rainy days making up a few and attributing them to Yogi. However adventurous he may have been with words and however awkward at times in expressing himself, Berra always knew what he was talking about. When it came to baseball, his I.Q., in the words of Casey Stengel, "was right up there with Mr. Einstein's."

In second place in the MVP voting was righthander Ned Garver, who won 20 games for the last-place St. Louis Browns, who lost 102. (It was no doubt the enchantment of winning 20 for a team of bumblers that allowed Garver to finish so high in the voting. Ned's achievement was more heroic than valuable). Yankee righthander Allie Reynolds was third.

Berra's 1951 Record

G	AB	HITS	2B	3B	HR	RUNS	RBI	SB	BAV
141	547	161	19	4	27	92	88	5	.294

Yogi Berra

1952: Bobby Shantz

After winning 18 games in 1951, Bobby Shantz "figured I'd have a good year in 1952..." Well, he did..."but [I] never expected it to be that good." The crucial change came when he learned how to take something off his fastball without slowing his arm speed. When he had mastered this subtle change in motion, he started winning. "Wow, did I start to win!" he said. "I got to a point where I could do just about anything I wanted to out there on the mound. Everything seemed to go right. I was changing speeds when I was behind the batter and throwing the ball right on the corner. You sometimes get into ruts where everything goes wrong, but this was the opposite—everything was going right."

At one point in the 1952 season, Bobby's record was 14-2. Later on he was 20-3, finishing with a 24-7 record. In being voted Most Valuable Player, Shantz beat out the Yankees' Allie Reynolds, who was 20-8, and their 20-year-old sophomore center fielder, Mickey Mantle, who finished third in the balloting.

Shantz, who stood just 5'6", started 33 games and completed 27 of them, averaging better than eight innings per start.

Despite a fourth-place finish, the Athletics had some of the league's standout performers. In addition to MVP Shantz, they had the Rookie of the Year in righthander Harry Byrd (15-15), as well as the batting champion in firstbaseman Ferris Fain (.327).

Late in the season, Shantz was struck on the left wrist by a pitched ball, suffering two broken bones. The following spring, in his first start, he tore a shoulder muscle, perhaps from favoring the wrist. Although he pitched in the big leagues until 1964, working for eight different clubs, he was never again the same dominant pitcher he had been in 1952.

Shantz' 1952 Record

WON	LOST	PCT.	G	GS	CG	INP	HITS	BB	SO	SH	ERA
24	7	.744	33	33	27	280	230	63	152	5	2.48

Bobby Shantz

1953: Al Rosen

Twenty-four baseball writers voted for the American League MVP in 1953, and all twenty-four had Al Rosen's name at the top of their ballot. It was a clean sweep for the Cleveland thirdbaseman, who was by far the league's dominant hitter in 1953, leading with 43 home runs (most ever by an American League thirdbaseman) and 145 runs batted in. He just missed a Triple Crown when Washington's Mickey Vernon edged him out on the last day of the season, .337 to .336.

Rosen had broken in with Cleveland in 1950, setting a league rookie record with 37 home runs (a record that stood until 1987), when Mark McGwire hit 49 for Oakland). An extremely tough, aggressive, and hard-nosed player, Rosen drove in over 100 runs during each of his first five seasons and averaged 31 homers per season. But then a badly broken finger impaired his batting grip and, rather than contend with decreasing performances, he retired after the 1956 season at the age of 31.

Despite Rosen's sensational slugging, the best the Indians could do was finish second to the Yankees, 8½ games behind. Yankee catcher Yogi Berra was a distant second to Al in the MVP tabulation and Vernon was third.

Rosen's 1953 Record

G	AB	HITS	2B	3B	HR	RUNS	RBI	SB	BAV
155	599	201	27	5	43	115	145	8	.336

Al Rosen, one of the few unanimous MVP selections.

1954: Yogi Berra

Despite winning the pennant with an American League record of 111 victories, the Cleveland Indians were unable to produce the Most Valuable Player in 1954. Cleveland players finished second, third, fifth, and sixth in the balloting: outfielder Larry Doby, the home run and RBI leader, was second; batting champion (.341) Bobby Avila was third; and 23-game winners Bob Lemon and Early Wynn were fifth and sixth, respectively.

The winner in a fairly close vote (230-210) was Yankee catcher Yogi Berra, taking the second of his three MVP trophies. Despite the surprise of the vote, Yogi was a most deserving winner, hitting 22 home runs, driving in 125 runs (one fewer than Doby), and batting .307. The tireless Berra caught 149 games, and when asked if he ever got tired, reportedly said, "I don't, but my body does." Another bit of Yogi's arcane wisdom went like this: "You've got to be very careful if you don't know where you are going, because you might not get there."

Together with predecessor Bill Dickey, Yogi gave the Yankees Hall of Fame representation behind the plate from 1929 through 1959, which is one reason the team took 18 pennants over that span.

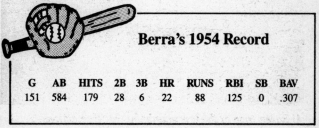

Berra's 1954 Record

G	AB	HITS	2B	3B	HR	RUNS	RBI	SB	BAV
151	584	179	28	6	22	88	125	0	.307

1955: Yogi Berra

For the first time since 1951, the American League MVP was a member of the pennant-winning club, and in each instance the man was Yogi Berra. The Yankee Rock of Gibraltar copped the award for the third time, with Detroit's Al Kaline (the 20-year-old batting champ, with a .340 average) in second place and Cleveland's Al Smith third. Yogi's teammate Mickey Mantle, who led the league with 37 home runs, was fifth, after Ted Williams.

Catching 145 games, winning a third MVP Award, Berra had by now established himself as one of the great catchers of all time.

"You never had to tell him anything twice," Casey Stengel said. "He was my ball club in those years. He held us together."

Despite the battering a man endures while catching a whole season, Berra continued to hit solidly, belting 27 home runs and driving in 108 runs, second best in the league. Always the positive thinker, Yogi once found his batting average taking a dive and responded thusly to a reporter who asked him to explain the slump: "I ain't in a slump, I just ain't hitting."

Between the retirement of DiMaggio in 1951 and the full blooming of Mantle in 1956, the star of baseball's greatest team was its durable, hard-hitting catcher.

Berra's 1955 Record

G	AB	HITS	2B	3B	HR	RUNS	RBI	SB	BAV
147	541	147	20	3	27	84	108	1	.272

Yogi Berra; along with Foxx, DiMaggio, and Mantle, a three-time MVP.

1956: Mickey Mantle

You could see it coming, right from the beginning, from the time he first appeared in the Yankees' spring training camp in 1951. He was an unknown 19-year-old who had never played higher than Class C Ball, but it was all there—the ground-burning running speed and the thunderous power from either side of the plate. For opposing pitchers, it was like a dark cloud casting an ever more ominous shadow upon their landscape. But for the New York Yankees, it was a golden sun climbing higher into the sky.

Though he did lead the league in homers in 1955, it wasn't until 1956 that Mickey Mantle exploded in full glory, turning in the most sustained display of power-hitting since the bruising days of Babe Ruth, Lou Gehrig, Jimmie Foxx, and Hank Greenberg.

Mickey became the sixth American Leaguer to win the Triple Crown, hitting 52 home runs, driving in 130 runs, and batting .353. In finally attaining the superstardom that had been predicted for him, the 24-year-old Oklahoman easily won the first of his three MVP Awards, finishing ahead of Yogi Berra and Detroit's Al Kaline.

In 1956, the youngster whom the Yankees had signed for a $1,150 bonus had 20 home runs by the end of May (a record), including one that had come within inches of being the first fair ball to be hit out of Yankee Stadium. He became one of the game's great drawing cards, both at home and on the road. Next to Ted Williams, he was baseball's most charismatic man at home plate.

"When I first saw him," his manager Casey Stengel

said, "I said I'd never seen anything like him. I thought maybe Cobb and Ruth had come back in the same body, but then I knew that wasn't possible. So I just kept watching him to see if I could finally believe what I was seeing. Now I've been watching him for six years I still haven't seen anything like it, but at least I can believe it."

That was Stengel's way of saying that Mantle was one of a kind.

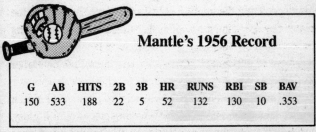

Mantle's 1956 Record

G	AB	HITS	2B	3B	HR	RUNS	RBI	SB	BAV
150	533	188	22	5	52	132	130	10	.353

Mickey Mantle

1957: Mickey Mantle

It was two MVP Awards in a row for Mickey Mantle and four in a row for Yankee players, as Mickey led the club to another pennant in 1957. Mickey batted a career high .365, but lost out on another batting crown when Ted Williams turned in a skyscraping .388 mark. Mickey hit 34 home runs and drove in 94 runs, and that relatively low RBI total indicated that the Yankee switch-hitting menace had become a victim of his own success—he was walked 146 times. It was a replay of the Ruth-Williams syndrome—why pitch to somebody whose mere appearance at home plate intimidated pitchers and who could be fooled on a pitch and still hit it where the grass doesn't grow?

Although he was to have some more highly productive years, Mantle's average never again was as lofty. As much a part of the Mantle legend as his gargantuan home runs were the many injuries, some nagging, some extremely serious, that began taking their toll in mid-career. He suffered enough breaks, pulls, tears, and sprains to make his medical chart read like a post-game NFL report. In addition, he enjoyed the night life, and if some reports are true, it's a wonder he didn't develop bone chips from bending his elbow.

Nevertheless, he was tough and stoic, playing through pain and injury with a gritty tolerance that won him universal respect. In winning his second MVP Award, Mickey beat out Williams by 24 votes. Washington's home run and RBI leader, Roy Sievers, came in third.

Mantle's 1957 Record

G	AB	HITS	2B	3B	HR	RUNS	RBI	SB	BAV
144	474	173	28	6	34	121	94	16	.365

Mickey Mantle

1958: Jackie Jensen

The Yankee grip on the MVP Award was finally broken in 1958, though there was a somewhat tenuous Yankee connection. The winner, Boston's Jackie Jensen, had come to the majors with the Yankees in 1950, but the talent-laden New Yorkers were unable to fit him into the lineup and traded him to Washington, who in turn dealt him to the Red Sox.

A strong, righthanded pull hitter, Jensen took advantage of Fenway's nearby left-field wall and became the league's premier RBI man in the late 1950's, leading the league in 1956, 1958, and 1959. A superb athlete (he had been a track star and All-American fullback at the University of California), Jensen won the MVP honor by beating out New York's 21-game winner Bob Turley and Cleveland's Rocky Colavito, who hit 41 home runs. Jackie had 35 home runs, 122 RBIs, and a .286 batting average, while playing an excellent right field for the Red Sox.

A year later, after another fine season, the 31-year-old star announced his retirement. His reasons were twofold: he admitted to a dislike of flying, and he did not like being separated from his wife and young children for so much of the time. Jensen did indeed sit out the 1960 season. He returned for the 1961 campaign, but then retired again, this time for good.

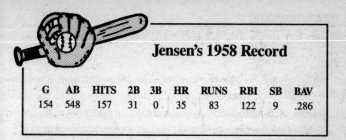

Jensen's 1958 Record

G	AB	HITS	2B	3B	HR	RUNS	RBI	SB	BAV
154	548	157	31	0	35	83	122	9	.286

Jackie Jensen

1959: Nelson Fox

Nelson Fox was an infield chatterbox, a non-stop hustler; he was a superb secondbaseman, a .300 hitter, and consistently the toughest man in the American League to strike out. He had a competitive zeal that often irritated the opposition, but his managers loved him.

"He was one of my favorites," said Paul Richards, who managed Fox in Chicago in the early 1950s. "He was only around five-eight, and you'd see those hard sliders like Mantle going into second base to break up a double play, but Foxie never gave an inch. He'd get knocked on his ass, but he'd make the play."

Fox was the heart and soul of the Go-Go Sox, those unlikely and unexpected pennant winners of 1959 (the first White Sox club to win a pennant since the 1919 band, who threw the World Series and have gone down in the history books with the Jesse James gang and the Harding Administration).

"We popgunned 'em to death," said White Sox player Billy Goodman, describing the Chicago attack that year.

With a .306 batting average and 191 hits, Fox spearheaded that modest attack, fanning just 13 times in 624 official at bats. In the field, the 31-year-old scrapper was in perpetual motion, leading secondbasemen in putouts (he did that for ten consecutive years), assists (he led six times) and fielding percentage (he did that seven times).

The White Sox were 1-2-3 in the MVP voting, with Fox on top, followed by shortstop Luis Aparicio and 22-game winner Early Wynn.

Fox's selection was popular among baseball people,

who appreciated the many contributions the little second-baseman made to winning a game. He bunted, he hit and ran, he slapped the ball to all fields, took the extra base, made the plays in the field, and drove the opposition to distraction.

"A great little player," Casey Stengel said. "A real pain in the ass."

Apparently it took several post-game shampoos to get Nelson Fox out of your hair.

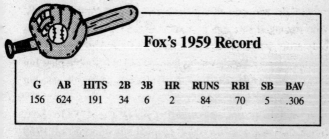

Fox's 1959 Record

G	AB	HITS	2B	3B	HR	RUNS	RBI	SB	BAV
156	624	191	34	6	2	84	70	5	.306

Nelson Fox

1960: Roger Maris

The New York Yankees reclaimed the MVP trophy in 1960 and would hold onto it for four years. The winner was a new man in town, outfielder Roger Maris, obtained in a winter deal with Kansas City, whose roster the Yankees had been raiding for several years, while a docile KC front office either looked the other way or looked not at all.

A lefthanded hitter with a power stroke that seemed expressly designed for Yankee Stadium's right field stands, Maris poled 39 home runs in his maiden voyage as a Yankee, driving in a league-leading 112 runs, batting .283 (his career high), and playing brilliantly in right field.

In winning the MVP Award, Maris narrowly edged teammate Mickey Mantle (who led the league with 40 homers) by a 225-222 count, with Baltimore third baseman Brooks Robinson pulling 211 votes for a close third-place finish.

With Yankee pitching falling off that year, the home run bats of Maris and Mantle helped carry the New Yorkers back to the top of the league after spending 1959 in the wings, while the White Sox won their surprise flag. Between them, Roger and Mickey had 79 home runs. A year later, they would make that look paltry.

Maris' 1960 Record

G	AB	HITS	2B	3B	HR	RUNS	RBI	SB	BAV
136	499	141	18	7	39	98	112	2	.283

Roger Maris

1961: Roger Maris

Roger Maris was a shy, modest young man who had grown up in Fargo, North Dakota. He had played big league ball in Cleveland and Kansas City before coming to New York. He found the limelight with an MVP season in 1960. But in 1961, the limelight turned to blinding klieg lights. As Maris began hitting home runs at a record-shattering pace that summer, the attention swelled and the pressure grew. He was accompanied by reporters, notebooks, tape recorders, cameras, and questions. Most of the questions asking the same thing: "Do you think you can do it?" "It" referred to breaking Babe Ruth's single-season home run record of 60.

Unused to the constant crush of reporters with their relentless question (how could it possibly be answered?), Maris grew confused and then surly, alienating segments of the press. When he hit his 40th homer in his 96th game, Roger was 24 games ahead of Ruth's 1927 pace and the furor around him began to grow to what seemed hysterical proportions. But besides the pressure and the slants of opposing pitchers, there were other burdens laid on Roger Maris in 1961.

That was the year when the American League expanded to ten teams and introduced the 162-game schedule. Those extra eight games soon created a headache for Maris; Commissioner Ford Frick declared that unless Maris broke Ruth's record in 154 games (the length of the old schedule) Roger's feat would have a separate entry in the record book. In addition, Mantle was putting on his own home run show. On September 1, Roger had 51, Mickey 48.

Roger Maris: 61 in '61.

Fueling the problem for Maris was Mantle's popularity versus Maris' status as relative newcomer. The crowds were openly pulling for Mantle, feeling that the former Triple Crown winner was a more seemly heir to Ruth.

Hobbled by injuries, Mantle soon fell out of the chase, ending the season with 54 home runs. Maris belted number 59 in the club's 155th game, number 60 a few days later. Then, at Yankee Stadium, on the last day of the season, he hit number 61 off Boston's Tracy Stallard, making Stallard a permanent entry on baseball's trivia lists.

Today the record books have two separate entries for the single-season home run record: Maris, 61, for the 162-game schedule; Ruth, 60, for the 154-game route. Lest anyone think Roger's achievement was in any way tainted, he hit those home runs in 1961, many moons ago, and no one has come close to him since.

With both Maris and Mantle having had such startling seasons, the MVP vote was avidly awaited. It was close: Roger 202, Mickey 198. Baltimore first basemen Jim Gentile, with 46 homers and 141 RBIs, was third.

Maris' 1961 Record

G	AB	HITS	2B	3B	HR	RUNS	RBI	SB	BAV
161	590	159	16	4	61	132	142	0	.269

A familiar scene in 1961: Mickey Mantle welcoming home Roger Maris after one of Roger's 61 home runs. The batboy is at left.

1962: Mickey Mantle

The Yankee grip on the MVP Award continued on in 1962, with Mickey Mantle winning for the third time. Injuries held Mantle to just 123 games, during which he hit 30 home runs, drove in 89 runs, and batted .321. These were solid numbers, though hardly attention-grabbers; it so happened, however, there were no truly dominant performers in the league that year. Yankee secondbaseman Bobby Richardson was runner-up in the voting and Minnesota's Harmon Killebrew was third. Harmon had 48 homers and 126 RBIs (both league-leading totals) and helped his club finish second in the ten-team single-division league, but his .243 batting average and frozen glove worked against him.

Roger Maris, MVP for the past two years, turned in a productive season with 33 homers, 100 RBIs, but just a .256 average. Anyway, it was clear by now that Mantle was the foundation and inspiration as far as the Yankees were concerned, that he was to them what DiMaggio had been decades before. Sadly, however, the constant erosion of injuries was rapidly bringing Mantle's years of thunder and glory to a premature end.

Some of the Yankee teams of the DiMaggio era were probably good enough to have won without Joe. This cannot be said of any of the Mantle-led Yankee teams. It was as simple as that: without Mickey, they could not have won, which is as basic a definition of MVP as you'll find.

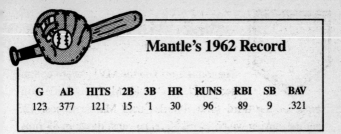

Mantle's 1962 Record

G	AB	HITS	2B	3B	HR	RUNS	RBI	SB	BAV
123	377	121	15	1	30	96	89	9	.321

Mickey Mantle. Those big sluggers always seem to be looking far after connecting.

1963: Elston Howard

With catcher Elston Howard winning in 1963, it gave the Yankees four consecutive MVPs and eight of the last ten (it would be 13 years before another Yankee won it). Howard had replaced the aging Yogi Berra behind the plate several years before, maintaining the Yankee tradition of outstanding catching that had begun with Bill Dickey in 1929.

Howard had joined the Yankees in 1955, the team's first black player. The club had been reluctant to sign blacks, and it wasn't until some pretty direct criticism had been leveled at them that they did. Club president George Weiss, a cold and humorless man who looked like he had been turned out by a taxidermist, claimed to be delighted with Howard because the black man was "quiet and gentlemanly." These were virtues indeed, but hitherto hardly the criteria for judging ballplayers. Otherwise, one assumes that Weiss would never have accepted such hearty characters as Ty Cobb, Babe Ruth and Dizzy Dean.

Howard batted .287, hit 28 home runs, and drove in 85 runs, which was just the kind of hitting the team had been getting from the position when Berra had been the regular. Finishing a distant second in the voting was Detroit's Al Kaline, with Howard's favorite pitcher, Whitey Ford (24-7 for the Yankees), coming in third.

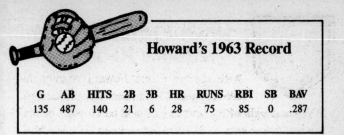

Howard's 1963 Record

G	AB	HITS	2B	3B	HR	RUNS	RBI	SB	BAV
135	487	140	21	6	28	75	85	0	.287

Elston Howard

71

1964:
Brooks Robinson

The Yankees won a fifth straight pennant in 1964, but did not turn out a fifth straight MVP, although they did have the runner-ups in Mickey Mantle and Elston Howard. The winner was Baltimore thirdbaseman Brooks Robinson, whose glove was the closest thing to a magic wand baseball has ever seen.

It was about Brooks that a Baltimore pitcher said, "Anything he does up at home plate is a bonus, because we don't care if he never gets a hit, as long as he's out there at third base every day."

After he had been in the big leagues for a few years, however, the Oriole pitchers had very little to complain about concerning Robinson's hitting; the modest and likable Arkansas native, in fact, won the American League's MVP Award in 1964 as much for his hitting as for his fielding.

Robinson would eventually play on four Baltimore pennant winners, but ironically the 1964 club was not among them. It was for a third-place Oriole team that Brooks put in his greatest season, batting .317 and driving in 118 runs (best in the league) and flashing that magnetic glove all summer long.

Was Brooks the greatest fielding thirdbaseman of all time? The question was put to Paul Richards, Baltimore's manager when Brooks first came to the majors.

"He's the best I've ever seen," Richards said, "and while I suppose it may be possible for somebody to be better, my feeling is that fellow would have to come from another planet."

Robinson was held in high esteem not only as a ball-player but also as a human being. In the words of one Baltimore sportswriter, "Brooks never asked anyone to name a candy bar after him. In Baltimore, people name their children after him."

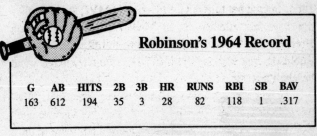

Robinson's 1964 Record

G	AB	HITS	2B	3B	HR	RUNS	RBI	SB	BAV
163	612	194	35	3	28	82	118	1	.317

Brooks Robinson, His glove inhaled everything that came third base way.

1965: Zoilo Versalles

By 1965, despite playing what many baseball people consider the key position on the field, only two shortstops had ever won the American League's MVP Award—Lou Boudreau in 1948 and Phil Rizzuto in 1950. Then, Minnesota's Zoilo Versalles had the year of his career and became the third, outpolling teammate and batting champion Tony Oliva and 1964's winner Brooks Robinson.

Helping to ignite the Twins to their first pennant, the 25-year-old Versalles led the league in runs (126), doubles (45), triples (12), and was the first shortstop in league history to lead in total bases (308). On the negative side, he also fanned more than anybody else (122) and led shortstops in errors (39).

Versalles was a fiery and exciting player in 1965—he outpolled Oliva, the batting champion (.321) and hit leader (185) by 101 votes—but it proved to be the 25-year-old shortstop's peak season. He batted .249 the next year and only .200 the following year. Then he began the melancholy wandering that attends a sliding career, playing for the Los Angeles Dodgers, Cleveland Indians, Washington Senators and Atlanta Braves. He left the big leagues in 1971.

Versalles' 1965 Record

G	AB	HITS	2B	3B	HR	RUNS	RBI	SB	BAV
160	666	182	45	12	19	126	77	27	.273

Zoilo Versalles: one spectacular year, and then...

Some truly spectacular fielding by Brooks Robinson helped the Baltimore Orioles defeat the Cincinnati Reds in the 1970 World Series. After the final game, Reds manager Sparky Anderson was being interviewed by the press. One reporter mentioned Robinson: " If someone threw a ball in the air right now, " Anderson said, "Robinson would come flying through the wall and catch it before it hit the floor."

1966: Frank Robinson

Having won MVP honors in the National League with the Cincinnati Reds in 1961, Baltimore's Frank Robinson became the only man in big league history to win the top award in both leagues when the writers made him their unanimous choice in 1966.

Not only did the Reds make a mistake of monumental proportions when they traded the 29-year-old slugger to the Orioles (for pitcher Milt Pappas) after the 1965 season, but the Cincinnati front office compounded it by describing Robinson as "an old twenty-nine." This goaded Robinson, who was already by nature a proud man and fiercely aggressive performer.

Robinson, who in 1975 would take over the Cleveland Indians as baseball's first black manager, was a natural leader on the field, and he did it by example. His playing style bordered on the belligerent: he defied pitchers by standing right on top of the plate; he rattled the bones of infielders as he slid to break up double plays; he constantly exhorted his teammates to do better.

In a generally weak-hitting year (the American League batted a collective .240), Robinson put together a smashing Triple Crown performance: 49 home runs, 122 RBIs, .316 batting average; he also led in runs, total bases, and slugging. It was a runaway performance.

The Orioles won the pennant and World Series, and also swept the top three slots in the MVP balloting, with Brooks Robinson and firstbaseman Boog Powell following Frank in the final tally.

Robinson's 1966 Record

G	AB	HITS	2B	3B	HR	RUNS	RBI	SB	BAV
155	576	182	34	2	49	122	122	8	.316

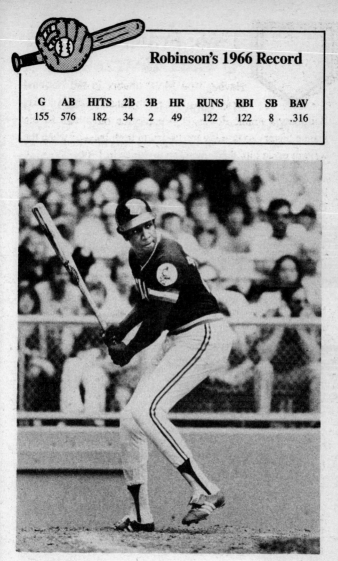

Frank Robinson

1967:
Carl Yastrzemski

His manager, Dick Williams, said that "in 1967 Carl Yastrzemski was the greatest ballplayer I ever saw."

It was the year of Boston's "Impossible Dream," and the man who wove more threads than any other into that ethereal tapestry was Yastrzemski, who hit and played left field as though his every move had been scripted by a fantasy-drunk Hollywood writer.

The Red Sox had finished ninth the year before, and there was little reason to expect much more in 1967. But driven by the caustic tongue and managerial genius of Williams and led by the seething play of Yastrzemski, the dream became a sublime reality.

By hitting 44 home runs, driving in 121 runs, and batting .326, Yastrzemski gave the American League its second Triple Crown winner in a row (Minnesota's Harmon Killebrew tied for the home-run lead) and its second straight runaway MVP—Killebrew and Detroit catcher Bill Freehan were distant runners-up.

Making Yastrzemski's performance more scintillating was the highly charged pressure of a pennant race that kept pinching tighter and tighter as the September days fell away. The more the tension built and the quicker the pulse beat became, the better he played. With the pennant in balance every day, Yastrzemski had 23 hits in his last 44 at bats, including 10 for his last 13, seven for his last eight, and four-for-four on the final day, when the Red Sox clinched the pennant.

How close had that pennant race been? Well, the White

Sox finished fourth, three games out, and Minnesota and Detroit each finished one game out and weren't eliminated until the final day. And the man who arranged all of that furniture was Carl Yastrzemski.

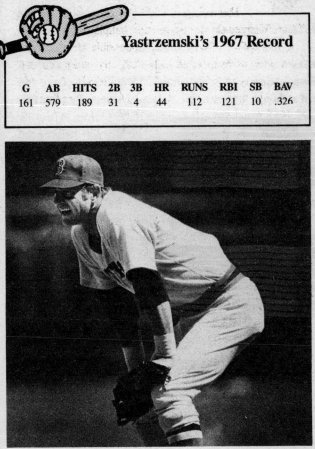

Yastrzemski's 1967 Record

G	AB	HITS	2B	3B	HR	RUNS	RBI	SB	BAV
161	579	189	31	4	44	112	121	10	.326

"Carl Yastrzemski in 1967 was the greatest ballplayer I ever saw."–Red Sox manager Dick Williams.

1968:
Denny McLain

Appropriately enough in "The Year of the Pitcher," when most big league bats turned to cornstalks and a 2-0 count was considered a rally, the American League's Most Valuable player was a pitcher. He was not just any old pitcher, but a 30-game winner (31-6 to be exact). There hadn't been a 30-gamer in the bigs since Dizzy Dean in 1934, and it had long been assumed that the breed was extinct. But then along came Denny.

Denny McLain was verbose, likeable and uninhibited. But he was also undisciplined and antagonistic. He was baseball's answer to the freedom of spirit and anti-authoritarian convulsions common across the land in the late '60s. Denny's saving grace was he could pitch; he not only had splendid stuff on the mound, but also had, according to one of his catchers, an uncanny "sixth sense" out there. He seemed always to know what to throw, when to throw it, and where.

Leading the Tigers to the pennant, he became the first American League pitcher to be voted MVP since Bobby Shantz in 1952; and it wasn't even close, Denny sailing in well ahead of Tiger catcher Bill Freehan and Red Sox outfielder Ken Harrelson.

Denny pitched as well as he talked in 1968, which was no small achievement. The 24-year-old righthander started 41 games, completed 28 and pitched a league-high 336 innings. His 1.96 ERA was gaudy, but in the Year of the Pitcher there were three others that were better (the league batted a timid .230).

Denny's MVP plaque was the second one in the family—his father-in-law was Lou Boudreau. Denny backed up his big season with 24 wins in 1969, but this fellow was programmed to self-destruct. It all started coming apart in 1970, starting with a sore arm; then a three-month suspension for alleged bookmaking activities; another suspension for reportedly packing a gun; and then another one for what was deemed in certain quarters a really serious offense—emptying a bucket of ice water on the heads of a couple of sportswriters.

Denny's comet turned into a Roman candle, and by 1972, the 28-year-old one-time toeplate genius was out of baseball. A decade later, he was in the cooler for filling a rap sheet with offenses like extortion, drug involvement, and other niceties unbecoming a 30-game winner.

McLain's 1968 Record

WON	LOST	PCT.	G	GS	CG	INP	HITS	BB	SO	SH	ERA
31	6	.838	41	41	28	336	241	63	280	6	1.96

Denny McLain: 31 wins and then a jet stream to oblivion.

1969:
Harmon Killebrew

A man of imposing physical strength, Harmon Killebrew was a home-run hitter in the classic mold—he made emphatic contact with the ball and sent it on long, one-way journeys. He hit 40 home runs in a season eight times; only Ruth did better and only Aaron as well.

In 1969, the first year of division play in the big leagues, the muscle man from Payette, Idaho, had his greatest season, helping the Minnesota Twins to a Western Division title and gaining for himself the MVP Award. He finished well ahead of a pair of Baltimore busters, Boog Powell and Frank Robinson.

Harmon's power numbers in 1969 were impressive—49 home runs and 140 RBIs, both league leaders. Even with that many big blasts, however, Killebrew barely won the home run title—Washington's Frank Howard had 48 and Oakland's young power plant Reggie Jackson parked 47. Pitchers were so wary of Harmon that they walked him 145 times, a total exceeded in American League history only by Ruth, Williams, and Mantle (and Eddie Yost, who cajoled them out of pitchers).

Killebrew's problem was in the field; the Twins didn't know where to play him, or rather where to hide him. They stationed him, at one time or another, at first, third, and left field, hoping the ball wouldn't find him. One writer said of Harmon, "He'll drop any ball he gets his hands on." Press box hyperbole, but it gives you an idea. Nevertheless, Harmon could have quoted Ted Williams, who said, "They don't pay me to catch fly balls, they pay me to hit." And that's exactly what the muscular Killebrew did, and what he hit was home runs, so frequently that he stands third on the list of home runs per at bat, behind Babe Ruth and Ralph Kiner.

Killebrew's 1969 Record

G	AB	HITS	2B	3B	HR	RUNS	RBI	SB	BAV
162	555	153	20	2	49	106	140	8	.276

Harmon Killebrew

1970: Boog Powell

Baltimore's economy-sized first baseman Boog Powell had turned in an excellent season in 1969 with 37 home runs, 121 RBIs, and a .304 batting average. Yet he finished second in the MVP voting to Harmon Killebrew. But the big man (6'4" and anywhere up to 260 pounds) kept right on hacking and in 1970 his 35 homers, 114 RBIs, and .297 average helped the Orioles to the pennant and earned him the big trophy.

Because a man of his great size was so congenial and fun-loving, Boog (his first name was John) was often described as "cuddly" and a "teddy bear;" but with a bat in his hand he was a man fiercely at work. He was a lefthanded power hitter, with a smooth, quick swing that could make a pitcher's best intentions disappear with blinding suddenness. And although hardly swift of foot, he could display an agility around first base that belied his size. The infield on those Baltimore pennant winners consisted of Powell, Davey Johnson at second, Mark Belanger at short, and Brooks Robinson at third—one of the most airtight inner alignments in baseball history.

"He was a great target to throw to at first base," Brooks Robinson said. "It was like throwing at a wall."

Well behind Boog in the MVP voting were Minnesotans Tony Oliva and Harmon Killebrew. It was the second time Tony had been runner-up.

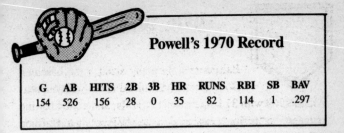

Powell's 1970 Record

G	AB	HITS	2B	3B	HR	RUNS	RBI	SB	BAV
154	526	156	28	0	35	82	114	1	.297

Boog Powell has the hometown fans roused up after parking one far and deep.

1971: Vida Blue

Vida Blue was virtually a rookie when he put on a blazing, summer-long show on the mound for the Oakland Athletics. The 21-year-old fastballing lefthander turned in a 24-8 record and was voted American League MVP, coming in well ahead of teammate Sal Bando and Baltimore's Frank Robinson.

Among Vida's achievements that year were 301 strike-outs, eight shutouts, and the league's best earned-run average, 1.82. Most people were astounded by the youngster's pitching. But those who had seen him when he briefly pitched for the A's the previous September had been given a glimpse of the future, for one of Vida's starts had resulted in a no-hitter over the hard-hitting Minnesota Twins.

Teaming with Catfish Hunter, Blue pitched the A's to the first of what would be five consecutive American League Western Division titles, a run that included three straight world championships.

Blue was remarkably mature and level-headed for one so young and so successful (his problems, oddly enough, came with maturity; in 1983 he was arrested on drug charges and later spent 90 days as a guest of the Federal Correctional Institute in Fort Worth). When Vida's employer, Charles Finley, offered Vida a few bucks if the youngster would change his name to "True" Blue, Vida told him to pickle the idea.

Blue's 1971 Record

WON	LOST	PCT.	G	GS	CG	INP	HITS	BB	SO	SH	ERA
24	8	.750	39	39	24	312	209	88	301	8	1.82

Vida Blue

1972: Dick Allen

When he came up with the Phillies in 1963, he was called Richie; later on in his career, he asked people to change it to Dick. But one thing he never changed was his free and independent attitude toward the things in baseball that annoyed him—like spring training, batting practice, getting to the ball park at the appointed time.

Allen shrugged off threats, fines and suspensions; and despite some spectacular hitting (no one ever questioned his hustle on the field), he soon found himself being traded from Philadelphia to St. Louis to Los Angeles. Then in 1972, he went over to the American League with the Chicago White Sox.

Allen hit the American League like thunder and lightning, winning the MVP Award in his first year there. A first-baseman now (he had come up as a thirdbaseman), Allen had a swing that detonated 37 home runs and drove in 113 runs, both league-leading marks, and batted .308. Part of Allen's success was attributed to the deft handling he received from manager Chuck Tanner, who allowed his tempermental star plenty of leeway, as long as Allen was there by game time.

With a three-year contract calling for $675,000, Allen was the highest-paid player of his time. But after his MVP season, the 30-year-old began a slow downhill slide that carried him out of the majors after the 1977 season.

In winning his trophy, Allen finished far ahead of Oakland outfielder Joe Rudi and Yankee relief ace Sparky Lyle.

Allen's 1972 Record

G	AB	HITS	2B	3B	HR	RUNS	RBI	SB	BAV
148	506	156	28	5	37	90	113	19	.308

Dick Allen

1973: Reggie Jackson

As far as Reggie Jackson was concerned, they selected the right man as MVP in the American League in 1973. Reggie never shortchanged himself in self-esteem. But it was okay, because two of the most abundant natural resources in baseball at the time were Reggie's ego and Reggie's talent. The ego was not offensively rampant; it was intelligently and entertainingly structured, while the talent, which included a spectacular flair for the dramatic, was there for the universe of baseball to see and appreciate.

Reggie would have been a star even without the spice of his engaging personality. He was the big slugger on Oakland's three consecutive world championships clubs of 1972-73-74, and 1973 was one of his finer summers. He led the league with 32 home runs and 117 RBIs, batting .293; and though it was forgotten in the latter stages of his 21-year career, as a young player he was a good outfielder with a strong throwing arm. Reggie was a unanimous MVP selection, finishing far ahead of Baltimore ace Jim Palmer and Kansas City outfielder Amos Otis.

No one ever ignored Reggie Jackson, not the fans, not the press, not teammates, opposition, no one. His employer in Oakland, Charles Finley, said of him, "He's no superstar except in his own eyes." His manager in New York, Billy Martin (whose own complex personality made him Reggie's natural enemy), had this to say of his star right fielder: "It's not that Reggie is a bad outfielder. He just has trouble judging the ball and picking it up."

When Reggie had a candy bar named after him in New

York, one sportswriter said it tasted like a hot-dog (hot-dog being baseball parlance for showoff). And George Steinbrenner, who had signed Dave Winfield to a $20 million dollar contract, made this gratuitous comparison between Dave and Reggie: "Dave's a good ballplayer, but not a superstar, not the way Reggie Jackson was."

The last word on Reggie, however, comes from the man himself. Commenting on the All-Star Game, he said, "I don't go there to compete. I go there to be seen."

Jackson's 1973 Record

G	AB	HITS	2B	3B	HR	RUNS	RBI	SB	BAV
151	539	158	28	2	32	99	117	22	.293

It looks like Reggie Jackson is about to make contact, right on the serious end of the bat.

1974: Jeff Burroughs

It was a comparatively slow year in the American League in 1974. Rod Carew did lead the league with a .364 batting average, but somehow Rod was always under-appreciated (he showed up seventh in the MVP balloting). Dick Allen led with 32 home runs and batted .301, but pulled only eight votes. Ferguson Jenkins won 25 for Texas and finished fifth, while Catfish Hunter won 25 for Oakland and finished sixth.

Three of Oakland's world champions finished second, third, and fourth—Joe Rudi, Sal Bando, and Reggie Jackson. The winner, and quite handily, was outfielder Jeff Burroughs of the Texas Rangers, who hit 25 home runs and batted .301, while leading the league with 118 RBIs. Although this was a good season, Burroughs was a surprise winner, particularly in the ease with which he had won (248 votes to 161 for runner-up Rudi).

Despite some productive seasons later in his career, the big, strong Burroughs never quite fulfilled the expectations baseball people held for him. While he did hit for power in 1975 and 1976, his batting averages shrank to .226 and .237, whereupon he was dealt to Atlanta, where in that club's congenial park he belted 41 homers. It was, however, his last flirtation with stardom.

Describing Burroughs' MVP Award in 1974, one sportswriter said, "He sort of sneaked in."

Burroughs' 1974 Record

G	AB	HITS	2B	3B	HR	RUNS	RBI	SB	BAV
152	554	167	33	2	25	84	118	2	.301

Jeff Burroughs

93

1975: Fred Lynn

In 1975, the Boston Red Sox brought up two truly outstanding rookies in their "Gold Dust Twins" outfielders, Fred Lynn and Jim Rice. Rice eventually went on to have the greater career, but in 1975 Lynn made one of the most emphatic debuts in baseball history.

The pennant-winning 1975 Red Sox were a team of stars, present and future, including Carl Yastrzemski, Rico Petrocelli, Rick Burleson, Dwight Evans, Carlton Fisk, and Cecil Cooper, along with Lynn and Rice. But the 23-year-old Lynn was the brightest of them all.

The handsome, sweet-swinging Southern Californian became the first man ever to win Rookie of the Year and Most Valuable Player honors in the same year. Lynn's fluid power swing dispatched 21 homers, a league-leading 47 doubles, drove in 105 runs, and batted .331. In addition, he played a superb center field, with a penchant for spectacular catches.

On June 18, against the Detroit Tigers in Tiger Stadium, Lynn had the night of his life, hitting three home runs, a triple, and single, tying an American League record with 16 total bases.

In winning the MVP Award, Lynn finished far ahead of Kansas City firstbaseman John Mayberry and teammate Rice.

Lynn's 1975 Record

G	AB	HITS	2B	3B	HR	RUNS	RBI	SB	BAV
145	528	175	47	7	21	103	105	10	.331

Fred Lynn, Rookie of the Year and MVP.

Toronto's George Bell was often surly and hostile to the press in 1987, and at other times would not even talk to them. A teammate said, "George lets his bat do the talking for him."

1976:
Thurman Munson

The 1976 winner of the American League Most Valuable Player Award was a Yankee catcher in the great tradition of Yankee catchers, which had begun with Bill Dickey and been carried forward by Yogi Berra and Elston Howard. Thurman Munson, as rugged and gritty a character as ever played baseball, was the hard-nosed force behind the Yankee pennant machine of 1976-77-78, and as lethal a clutch hitter as Berra had been.

There was nothing graceful about Munson. He seemed born into a dirty uniform. His teammates, who held him in high esteem, called him "squatty body" for his powerful, compact appearance. He could be moody and sullen, and certain journalists were frankly intimidated by him.

Munson was an easy winner in the MVP voting, finishing far ahead of Kansas City's young thirdbaseman George Brett and Munson's Yankee teammate Mickey Rivers. The 29-year-old Munson batted .302, and it was a hard .302—he drove in 105 runs. (Since 1939, only three American League catchers had driven in 100 or more runs in a season, and all had been Yankees—Dickey, Berra and Munson).

When Reggie Jackson joined the Yankees in 1977 and immediately announced that he and not Munson was "the straw that stirs the drink," Thurman was stung and thereafter sullenly tolerated his outspoken teammate.

On August 2, 1979, Munson's life was cut suddenly and brutally short. It was an off day for the Yankees and he was at the Canton, Ohio, airport practicing touch-and-go landings in his recently purchased Cessna Citation. The plane crashed. Neither of his two passengers were seriously injured, but Munson died on impact. He was 32 years old.

Munson's 1976 Record

G	AB	HITS	2B	3B	HR	RUNS	RBI	SB	BAV
152	616	186	27	1	17	79	105	14	.302

Thurman Munson

1977: Rod Carew

By 1977, Rod Carew had won five batting crowns, but had never come close to being voted MVP. That year the Minnesota firstbaseman was not to be denied, finishing comfortably ahead of Kansas City's Al Cowens and Baltimore's Ken Singleton. Carew, the man of many batting stances and the uncanny eye, entertained baseball America by flirting with a .400 batting average throughout most of the summer. He wound up with a snow-capped .388, highest since Ted Williams had turned in a similar mark in 1957.

With a punch-and-slap style that was anomalous in the free-swinging age in which he played, Carew rang up an enormous total of 239 hits, most in the American League since 1928. Despite being a contact hitter, Carew still had 68 extra base hits—38 doubles, 16 triples and 14 home runs.

Los Angeles Times writer Jim Murray had this to say of the Carew batting style: "Watching Rod Carew bat is like watching Bulova make a watch, DeBeers cut a diamond …Rod Carew doesn't make hits, he composes them." Indeed, the Carew bat was like a maestro's wand, cajoling the pitcher into coughing up a line drive.

But not even Carew—who won seven batting titles in his career—was immune to the nitpickers. They said all he did was get hits, that he didn't drive in runs. These people were the cultural descendants of those who said that all Walter Johnson had was a fastball and all Caruso could do was sing.

Carew's 1977 Record

G	AB	HITS	2B	3B	HR	RUNS	RBI	SB	BAV
155	616	239	38	16	14	128	100	23	.388

Rod Carew

1978: Jim Rice

The question arose again in 1978: who is more valuable to a team, the pitcher who has a brilliant season or the everyday player who has a brilliant season? Prompting the question was the 25-3 record of Yankee lefthander Ron Guidry and the awesome slugging of Red Sox outfielder Jim Rice. The baseball writers filed their verdict that fall: Rice 352 votes, Guidry 291 (Milwaukee outfielder Larry Hisle was third).

It wasn't Rice's fault that the Red Sox dissipated what on July 17 was a 14-game lead over the Yankees. In the midst of one of the most thunderous slugging careers in recent decades, the Boston powerhouse led the league with 46 home runs, 15 triples, 139 runs batted in, 213 hits, .600 slugging average, and 406 total bases (he was the first American Leaguer since DiMaggio in 1937 to pile up 400 total bases). Despite being the Fenway Park left-field heir to Ted Williams and Carl Yastrzemski and despite his own prodigious slugging, Rice never enjoyed the same popularity as his predecessors. An intensely private man, wary of the press and ill at ease with strangers, he seemed content to remain broodingly within "fortress Rice."

Rice's reputation includes tales of his awesome physical strength. There is the story of a bat being broken in two by a checked swing. These are the kinds of stories that lose audiences for reminiscing grandfathers. But this particular story happens to be true. Ask the thirdbaseman who had to dance out of the way of the spinning bat head.

Rice's 1978 Record

G	AB	HITS	2B	3B	HR	RUNS	RBI	SB	BAV
163	677	213	25	15	46	121	139	7	.315

Jim Rice

1979: Don Baylor

California's Don Baylor was the American League MVP in 1979, the first Angels player to be so designated, and the voting wasn't even close—Baylor finished far ahead of Baltimore's Ken Singleton and Kansas City's George Brett.

An injured throwing arm was forcing Baylor more and more into a designated hitter status, a role the proud, hard-playing competitor resented and resisted. But it hardly affected his performance at home plate, where he had a sound and solid season, the best, in fact, of a long career. Never a man who hit for high average, "Donnie" (as his teammates called him) batted .296, smashed 36 home runs, and drove in a league-leading 139 runs (coincidentally, the same amount achieved by 1978's MVP Jim Rice).

Known for his ruggedness, Baylor suffered a variety of nagging injuries during the season, but still never missed a game. No one broke up a double play with more bone-crushing impact. His slides, however, were always clean. And no one was more fearless at home plate, where Baylor crowded close and refused to be intimated by inside pitches. As a result, he set records for being hit by pitches. In the case of most hit batters, the ball would strike them and drop to the ground; with Baylor, according to one observer, "the ball seems to bounce off him, like it's hitting a concrete wall."

As the years passed, Baylor's reputation as a team leader and positive clubhouse influence grew, adding immeasurably to his value. He also had to be counted as a winner, having played on championship clubs in Baltimore, California, Boston, Minnesota, and Oakland.

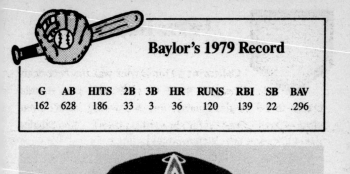

Baylor's 1979 Record

G	AB	HITS	2B	3B	HR	RUNS	RBI	SB	BAV
162	628	186	33	3	36	120	139	22	.296

Don Baylor

103

1980: George Brett

In 1980, at the All-Star break, George Brett was batting in the .330s. After that, he dug in and started to do some serious hitting, to the point where people began to ask whether he could do it. "It" referred to a .400 batting average, that magical hitting peak that had gone unvisited since Ted Williams had scaled it with a .406 mark in 1941. Brett's charge at .400 lasted longer than Rod Carew's in 1977, as George maintained the pace into late August. But then, between the intense scrutiny of the media (every Brett at-bat became an event) and some nagging injuries, George slipped into a mini-slump, then finished strong and checked in at the end with a .390 average, the best since Williams' and five hits short of .400.

Brett's .390 average belied an injury-dented season for the Kansas City thirdbaseman. He missed 45 games, most of them in the early going, so that when he began to blaze in July and August and three-and four-hit games became commonplace, his relatively low number of at-bats allowed his average to soar.

It was a George Brett year surely; his titanic three-run homer against the Yankees' Goose Gossage cinched the pennant for the Royals in the league championship series. George continued to be news in the World Series, when he suffered from a widely publicized hemorrhoidal condition. It allowed the whimsical Brett to say, "My problems are behind me."

Brett's 1980 season saw him drive home 118 runs in 117 games and win slugging honors with a .664 percentage. Brett's classic campaign overshadowed an extraordinary season by Milwaukee's Cecil Cooper, who batted .352 and had

219 hits; and one by George's teammate Willie Wilson, who batted .326 and had 230 hits. Nevertheless, the runner-ups in the MVP voting were a pair of Yankees, Reggie Jackson and Goose Gossage, followed by Wilson and Cooper.

Brett's 1980 Record

G	AB	HITS	2B	3B	HR	RUNS	RBI	SB	BAV
117	449	175	33	9	24	87	118	15	.390

George Brett

1981: Rollie Fingers

The 1981 season was baseball's strike season, when labor-management disputes gouged the heart out of the schedule. Fully one third of the games remained in their eggshells. Later on, the baseball establishment came up with the crackpot idea of a split season and a double-tiered playoff to determine the pennant winners.

Nevertheless, enough games were played to create a semblance of a season, and in the end the Milwaukee Brewers' Rollie Fingers emerged as MVP in the American League. Oakland's Rickey Henderson was a close second and Boston's Dwight Evans a distant third.

In the early 1970s, Fingers had been the ace reliever on Oakland's three championship clubs. Many people believed, some Oakland players included, that Rollie had been the one indispensable man on those teams.

In 1981, Fingers was working for the Milwaukee Brewers and he pitched brilliantly. Despite the fracture in the season, Rollie accumulated 28 saves and posted a miniscule 1.04 earned run average for 78 innings of work.

Fingers will probably be remembered as much for the esthetics of his waxed and wiry mustache as for his extraordinary late-inning missions to the mound (Rollie had, said one writer, a better record at saves than John the Baptist). He was the first American League relief pitcher ever accorded MVP honors.

Fingers' 1981 Record

WON	LOST	PCT.	G	GS	CG	INP	HITS	BB	SO	SH	ERA
6	3	.667	47	0	0	78	55	13	61	0	1.04

Rollie Fingers, mustache and all.

107

1982: Robin Yount

On the last day of the 1982 season, the Milwaukee Brewers were playing the Baltimore Orioles in the game that would decide the Eastern Division winner. Brewer shortstop Robin Yount rose to the challenge to say the least. He hit two home runs and a triple, as the Brewers ran off with a 10-2 victory. This was the kind of clutch performance you expected from a runaway MVP selection, as indeed Yount was in 1982 (with Baltimore's Eddie Murray and California's Doug DeCinces far behind).

The 27-year-old Yount was in his ninth big-league season and he made it his greatest, emerging as one of the most precious of baseball commodities, a good fielding, hard-hitting shortstop. As the class act of an especially hard-hitting club (216 home runs), Yount turned in a season of relentless consistency. He lead with 210 hits and 46 doubles, hit 29 homers, drove in 114 runs, batted .331, and

---

A writer was listening to former Yankee manager Joe McCarthy extol the many ball-playing virtues of his former center fielder Joe DiMaggio. Joe could hit, McCarthy said, hit with power, field, run, throw. Everything. There wasn't anything DiMaggio couldn't do on a ball field. He was "the perfect player."

Whimsically, the writer asked, "Tell me, Mr. McCarthy, could this perfect player of yours bunt?"

McCarthy smiled, "I don't know," he said, "nor did I ever have any intention of finding out."

lead in slugging (.578) as well as total bases (367). He was the first shortstop ever to lead the American League in slugging and the second to lead in total bases (Zoilo Versalles had done it in 1965).

In 1985, arm problems prevented Yount from playing shortstop and the Brewers shifted him to center field, where he continued to play with his own special radiance.

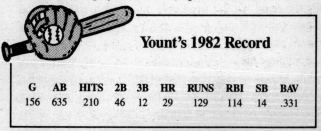

Yount's 1982 Record

G	AB	HITS	2B	3B	HR	RUNS	RBI	SB	BAV
156	635	210	46	12	29	129	114	14	.331

Robin Yount, about to get his man at second base.

1983: Cal Ripkin

The choice of Baltimore's Cal Ripkin in 1983 made it two MVP shortstops in a row. On top of that, he turned in a season that had an uncanny resemblance to that of Robin Yount's the year before. The 22-year-old Oriole batted .318, hit 27 home runs, 47 doubles, had 211 hits, scored 121 runs, and drove in 102, leading the league in runs, hits, and doubles.

It was a world championship season for the Orioles, underscored by the fact that Ripkin and teammate Eddie Murray ran a close one-two in the MVP voting, with White Sox catcher Carlton Fisk finishing third.

Few players had ever enjoyed so glittering, successful, and honor-laden an introduction to the big leagues as Cal Ripkin Jr. (son of the club's third-base coach). In 1982, the youngster had been voted the Rookie of the Year. Then in 1983 his splendid all-around performance helped take his team to a division title, pennant, and world championship.

A hallmark of the Ripkin style in this and following years was durability. He played a position that was vulnerable to injury, and remained out there game after game, year after year, building a consecutive game streak that would reach unique proportions during the 1988 season—over 1,000 games.

Ripkin's 1983 Record

G	AB	HITS	2B	3B	HR	RUNS	RBI	SB	BAV
162	663	211	47	2	27	121	102	0	.318

Mickey Cochrane was noted for his ruggedness behind home plate. The Athletics' catcher also had a certain possessiveness about the home plate area. One day a White Sox outfielder was barreling down the line, trying to score on what was going to be a close play. Cochrane, guarding the plate, took the throw from the outfield and braced himself as the runner tried to bowl him over. "It was like hitting a brick wall," one observer said, "The guy fell off to one side as Cochrane made the tag and never budged, despite a pretty good hit." Cochrane then turned to the sprawled runner and said, "That's what you get for trying to break into my house."

Cal Ripkin

1984:
Willie Hernandez

Following Rollie Fingers in 1981, Detroit's lefthanded reliever Willie Hernandez became in 1984 the next bullpen artist to carry off MVP recognition.

As the relief star of a club that was virtually unbeatable for the first six weeks of the 1984 season (the Tigers shot out to a 35-5 record), Hernandez gave a performance that was not only stunning but wholly unexpected. Acquired from the Phillies in a spring transaction, Willie had pitched ably but hardly memorably for seven years in the National League.

Willie's assortment of pitches, notably his fastball and elusive screwball, baffled American League batters to the extent that he became nearly unhittable and monotonously successful. Inserted into 33 save opportunities, he converted 32 of them, appearing in a total of 80 games, a league high. In 140 innings, he yielded just 96 hits, a remarkable ratio. His strikeouts-to-walks ratio was equally impressive—112-36.

Hernandez was a fairly easy winner in the MVP balloting, coming in ahead of Minnesota firstbaseman Kent Hrbek by 58 votes. Kansas City reliever Dan Quisenberry (with 44 saves) was third. Finishing a surprising fifth, after Eddie Murray, was the Yankees' Don Mattingly, who had 207 hits and led the league with a .343 average.

Hernandez' 1984 Record

WON	LOST	PCT.	G	GS	CG	INP	HITS	BB	SO	SH	ERA
9	3	.750	80	0	0	140	96	36	112	0	1.92

Willie Hernandez

113

1985: Don Mattingly

By 1985, the consensus among baseball people was that the game's greatest all-around player is Yankee first baseman Don Mattingly. That year Mattingly received the ultimate seal of approval, the Most Valuable Player Award. When one considers the quality of the first five players in the voting, it emphasizes how spectacular a year Mattingly had: following the Yankee first baseman were George Brett (.335 average), Rickey Henderson (80 stolen bases), Wade Boggs (240 hits, .368 average), and Eddie Murray (124 RBIs).

Mattingly's year was reminiscent of the thunderous seasons put together a half-century before by another Yankee firstbaseman, Lou Gehrig. The 23-year-old Indianan hit 35 home runs, led the league with 48 doubles and 145 RBIs, had 211 hits and batted .324. In addition, he played a superb first base, leading league first basemen in fielding percentage with a .995 mark.

Mattingly had been a baseball standout on his Evansville, Indiana high school team, both as a pitcher and a hitter. Some big league scouts were interested in signing the youngster as a pitcher, but Mattingly had other ideas.

"I didn't want to pitch," he said. "I was a hitter."

To paraphrase Shakespeare—it's a wise young man who knows himself.

⚾

Mattingly's 1985 Record

G	AB	HITS	2B	3B	HR	RUNS	RBI	SB	BAV
159	652	211	48	3	35	107	145	2	.324

Don Mattingly

115

1986: Roger Clemens

It was another year of sumptuous achievement for Don Mattingly in 1986: league-
leading 238 hits, league-leading 53 doubles, 31 home runs,
113 runs batted in, .352 batting average, league-leading .573
slugging average, league-leading 388 total bases. But it was
also the year of Boston's Roger Clemens, who fireballed the
Red Sox to the pennant with a 24-4 record, striking out 237
and posting the best ERA, 2.48. Along the way, he set a new
one-game strikeout record when he fanned 20 Seattle Mari-
ners at Fenway Park on April 29.

So it became one of baseball's classic post-season argu-
ments: who is more valuable, the great pitcher or the great
everyday player? With "most valuable" never having been
precisely defined, the argument, circa 1986, was for the
moment settled by the MVP balloting: Clemens 339, Mattingly 258 (Roger's teammate Jim Rice was third).

When the writers put Clemens' record to close scrutiny, they saw that 14 of Roger's wins followed Red Sox
defeats, meaning that with the big righthander in the rota-
tion, it was most improbable for the team to suffer a pro-
longed losing streak.

Clemens opened the season with 14 straight wins and
kept going until the MVP trophy was in his firm embrace.

Clemens' 1986 Record

WON	LOST	PCT.	G	GS	CG	INP	HITS	BB	SO	SH	ERA
24	4	.857	33	33	10	254	179	67	238	1	2.48

Roger Clemens, Boston's "Rocket Man."

1987: George Bell

The baseball writers gave a commendable display of objectivity in 1987 when they voted Toronto outfielder George Bell the Most Valuable Player Award. Bell was moodily taciturn when the writers were around, and sometimes downright hostile. Nevertheless, when the MVP ballots had all been counted, Bell was the winner. The vote, however, was a close one, with Detroit shortstop Alan Trammell (who many people thought should have won) coming in a close second. Minnesota's Kirby Puckett was third.

When Bell stepped up to the plate that year, the ball seemed immune to the laws of gravity. He turned in a season of heavyweight slugging, with 47 home runs and 134 runs batted in, the latter figure a league high. (Oakland rookie first baseman Mark McGwire topped Bell and everyone else with 49 homers.) Twenty American League players had 30 or more home runs that year.

The talented, temperamental Bell hailed from San Pedro de Macoris in the Dominican Republic, that small, miracle town with a great natural resource of big-league ballplayers—Bell, Julio Franco, Tony Fernandez, Rafael Ramirez, Manny Lee, Pedro Guerrero, Mariano Duncan, Juan Samuel, and others.

Bell's 1987 Record

G	AB	HITS	2B	3B	HR	RUNS	RBI	SB	BAV
156	610	188	32	4	47	111	134	5	.308

George Bell

1988: Jose Canseco

By the beginning of July, the sportswriters were already tabbing Oakland's Jose Canseco as the American League's Most Valuable Player. By the end of the season, the Oakland muscle man had done nothing to dispel the praise; indeed, he had done enough to warrant being a unanimous selection (followed in the voting by Boston's Mike Greenwell, Minnesota's Kirby Puckett, and New York's Dave Winfield—four outfielders right at the top).

Canseco, who had been Rookie of the Year in 1986, helped power the Athletics to their first pennant since 1974, and he did it with a flair seldom demonstrated by sluggers. He hit 42 home runs and stole 40 bases, thereby becoming the founding member of the "40–40" club. He also drove in 124 runs and painted it all prettier with a .307 batting average.

With home run totals of 33, 31, and 42 in his first three seasons, Canseco became the first man in big league history to hit 30 or more home runs in each of his first three years in the big leagues. And not only did this fellow hit home runs, but he put some real mileage on many of them.

"The scary thing about Canseco," one American League manager said during the season, "is he's only 24 years old."

Canseco's 1988 Record

G	AB	HITS	2B	3B	HR	RUNS	RBI	SB	BAV
158	610	187	34	0	42	120	124	40	.307

Jose Canseco

121

About the Author

Don Honig is one of America's best-known and prolific baseball historians. He is the author of 25 books about the national pastime, including *Baseball When the Grass Was Real*, *Baseball Between the Lines*, *Baseball America*, plus histories of the National League, the American League, the World Series, the All-Star Game, the New York Yankees, the New York Mets and the Los Angeles Dodgers. Mr. Honig is also the author of *The Donald Honig Reader* and has written over 30 baseball titles for young readers. He lives in Cromwell, Connecticut.